SCIENCE WORKSHOP

WATER·PADDLES & BOATS

Pam Robson

Gloucester Press

NEW YORK LONDON TORONTO SYDNEY

© Aladdin Books 1992

First published in
the United States in 1992 by
Gloucester Press
95 Madison Avenue
New York, NY 10016

Library of Congress Cataloging-in-Publication Data

Robson, Pam.
    Water, paddles, and boats / by Pam Robson.
    p. cm. — (Science workshop)
    Includes index.
    Summary: Suggests projects to explore the
properties of water and ways of putting them
to use for floating and energy.
    ISBN 0-531-17376-3
    1. Water-power—Juvenile literature. 2. Water
—Juvenile literature. 3. Water-power—
Experiments—Juvenile literature. [1. Water—
Experiments. 2. Water power—Experiments.
3. Experiments.] I. Title. II. Series.
    TC146.R63
    1992 627—dc20
    92-375   CIP   AC

CONTENTS

Design	David West
	Children's Book Design
Editors	Catherine Warren,
	Michael Flaherty
Designer	Stephen Woosnam Savage
Picture Researcher	Emma Krikler
Illustrator	Ian Moores
Consultant	Caroline Pontefract

PHOTOCREDITS
All the pictures in this book have been taken by Roger Viltos
apart from the pictures on pages: 6 top left and top right, 16 top
left, 24 top and 30 top left and top right: Eye Ubiquitous; 8 top left,
10 top, 22 top left and top right, 26 top left and 28 top: Spectrum
Colour Library; page 14 top left: U.S. Navy Sky Photos; page 20
top: C.O.I. Photos.

INTRODUCTION

Water is familiar to us all, yet it has some strange and beautiful properties. It can stretch and curve. It occurs naturally as solid, liquid, and gas. Sometimes it flows uphill. Most substances contract when cooled, whereas water expands. Thus an ice cube fills more space than it did before freezing. At boiling point, 212 F, water turns to steam, but it requires a large amount of heat for this transformation. Hence, water can store plenty of energy. Harnessed water power is a priceless resource in an age when people must conserve fuel. From the simple wooden waterwheel, engineers developed the water turbine and the steam turbine. These gigantic machines operate generators that provide us with hydroelectric power and sufficient propulsion to drive huge oil tankers. The unharnessed power of water has shaped the face of the earth since time began, carving valleys and coastlines, reshaping and dissolving rocks – even transporting them. The terrible force of tidal waves can unleash devastation on coastal communities. Water covers almost three-quarters of our planet. Made of hydrogen and oxygen, it is the most common compound of basic elements. However simple, plentiful yet precious, water is essential to all living things.

Introduction

Why it Works explaining the science ideas

Bright Ideas for further projects

Science projects with practical experiments

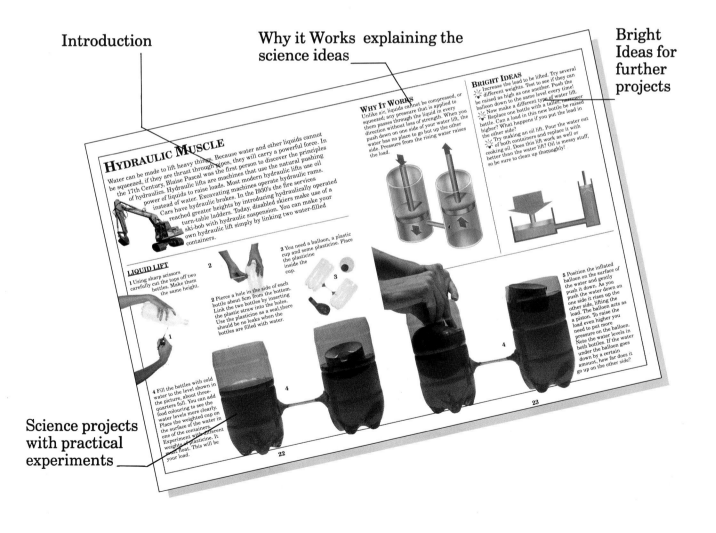

THE WORKSHOP

A science workshop is a place to test ideas, perform experiments, and make discoveries. To prove many scientific facts you don't need a lot of fancy equipment. In fact, everything you need for a basic workshop can be found around your home or school. Read through these pages and then use your imagination to add to your "home laboratory." Make sure that you are aware of relevant safety rules and look after the environment. A science experiment is an activity that involves the use of certain basic rules to test a hypothesis. A qualitative approach involves observation. A quantitative approach involves measurement. Remember, one of the keys to being a creative scientist is to keep experimenting. This means experimenting with equipment to give you the most accurate results, as well as experimenting with ideas. In this way, you will build up your workshop as you go along.

Making the Models
Before you begin, read through all the steps. Then make a list of the things you need and gather them together. Next, think about the project so that you have a clear idea of what you are about to do. Finally, take your time in putting the pieces together. You will find that your projects work best if you wait while glue dries or water heats. If something goes wrong, retrace your steps. And, if you can't fix it, start over. Every scientist makes mistakes, but the best ones know when to begin again!

General Tips
There are at least two parts to every experiment: experimenting with materials and testing a science "fact." If you don't have all the materials, experiment with others instead. For example, try a plastic soda bottle if you can't find a dishwashing liquid container. Once you've finished experimenting, read your notes thoroughly and think about what happened, evaluating your measurements and observations. See what conclusions you can draw from your results.

Safety Warnings
Make sure an adult knows what you are doing at all times. Many of these projects are made from plastic bottles. Make sure you don't use flammable materials, like plastic, where heating is involved. Always be very careful when cutting them with scissors. If you spill any water, wipe it up right away. Slippery surfaces can be dangerous. Clean up your workshop when you finish!

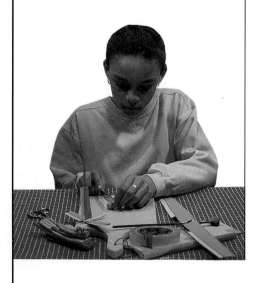

5

WATER'S CYCLE

Whether falling from a storm cloud or spurting from a kitchen sink, water moves in an endless cycle between Earth and sky. Year after year, the sun performs a fantastic feat, its energy evaporating 95,000 cubic miles of water from oceans, rivers, lakes, and streams. Rain and snow deliver this water back to Earth. The water cycle is this chain of evaporation and condensation, where water turns to vapor and back to liquid again. Heat accelerates evaporation; cooling leads to condensation. You can illustrate this cycle using hot water and ice.

CLOUDBURST

6

1 Clean a plastic soda bottle and remove the label. With scissors, carefully cut off the neck and make a wide opening down one side. The opening must be big enough for ice cubes. (Put these in last.)

1

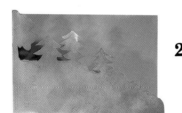

2

6 Place an aluminum foil dish inside the bottom of the cereal box as shown. Fill the dish with hot water from a kettle. Be careful!

2 From an empty cereal box cut out the forested mountain slope shown here. Make the front tree section lower than the rear sky section. Paint the scene to look like a real mountainside.

3 Make sure that the bottle fits inside the box as shown. It will be your cloud.

5

5 Place another sturdy box behind your mountainscape. (It should be the same height.) Tape the wire "handles" to the top of the box.

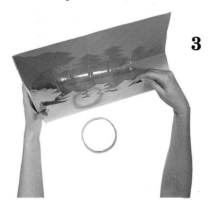

3

4

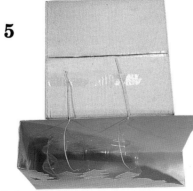

4 Ask a grown-up to cut a wire coat hanger into two lengths. Curve each piece of wire to fit around the plastic bottle. These metal loops will support the ice-filled bottle.

WHY IT WORKS

The sun's heat (1) fills molecules, or tiny particles, of surface water with energy, causing them to rise from the mass of water and escape into the air as water vapor (2). Trapped in the cool air, they condense around dust particles as droplets of water. These droplets join as the air cools, forming clouds (3). When the drops become too big and heavy to stay in the air, rain falls (4). The rainwater runs off the land back into the sea in rivers and streams (5).

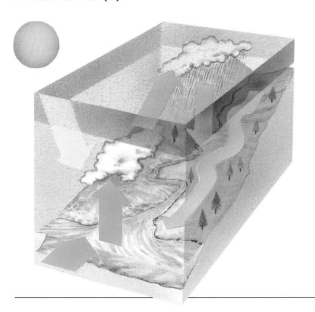

BRIGHT IDEAS

🔅 Measure rainfall with a rain gauge. Carefully cut the top off a dishwashing liquid bottle and set it upside down inside the bottom half like a funnel. Mark 1/8- or 1/16-inch divisions from the bottom of the container. Stand it outside in an exposed place. Keep a daily record - remember to empty the gauge every time.

🔅 Take two bowls filled to the brim with water. Stand one in a sunny place, the other in the shade. Compare the water levels at the end of each day to measure evaporation.

7

7 As the water evaporates from the dish, water vapor will rise and cool. As it cools, it will condense on the plastic ice-filled bottle. Rain will fall!

FREEZING AND MELTING

Not only does water appear as liquid and vapor, but if cooled to freezing point, water turns into a solid. Unlike most substances which shrink when they turn from liquid to solid, water expands. Water is more dense than ice. This is demonstrated by pipes which burst through the expansion of freezing water. Icebergs also give a good clue to the freezing and melting of water. These huge islands of ice adrift in Polar seas have broken off into the sea from vast glaciers or rivers of ice. As ice is 10 percent less dense than water, the top of an iceberg is only one tenth of the total size of the iceberg. The project below shows how ice floats and how water behaves as it melts.

MELTING ICEBERG

1 Clean a plastic soda bottle and remove the label. With a sharp pair of scissors carefully cut off the top.

4 Pour hot tap water into the large plastic bottle. Add a different coloring and stir.

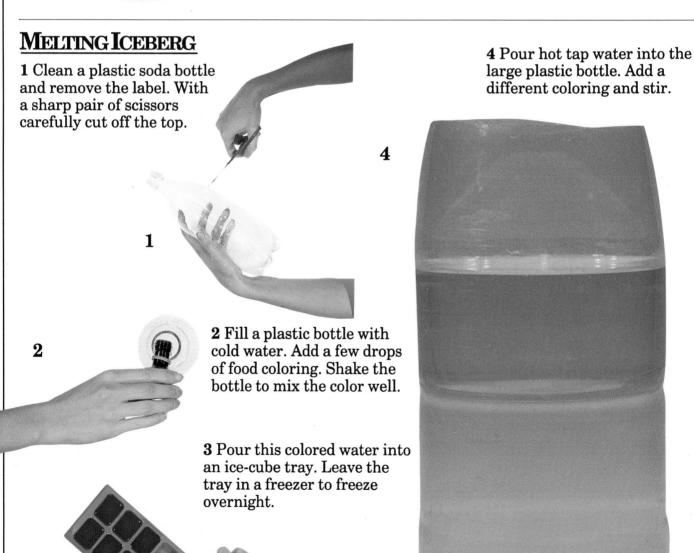

1

4

2 Fill a plastic bottle with cold water. Add a few drops of food coloring. Shake the bottle to mix the color well.

2

3 Pour this colored water into an ice-cube tray. Leave the tray in a freezer to freeze overnight.

3

WHY IT WORKS

When the ice cube melts, the water sinks as it regains its original density. Also, cold water is denser, or heavier, than hot water and sinks below it. This also causes the cold water melting from the ice cube to sink first to the bottom of the bottle.

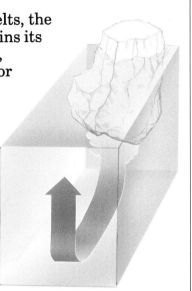

BRIGHT IDEAS

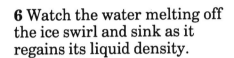

Fill a small plastic bottle to the brim with water and place it uncovered in the freezer. Wait for the water to freeze. See which takes up more space, the same quantity of liquid water or the frozen water. Try to measure the difference.

Float an ice cube in a full glass of water. See if the glass overflows as the ice melts.

5 Drop a colored ice cube in the hot water. Since ice is less dense than water it will float.

6 Watch the water melting off the ice swirl and sink as it regains its liquid density.

5

6

SALTY SOLUTIONS

Most water on the earth's surface is salty from minerals washed out of rocks by pounding rain and rushing rivers. One such mineral is sodium chloride, or common salt. Salt water is buoyant, which means it can hold things up. It helps boats to float better than they would in fresh water. Israel's Dead Sea, pictured here, is too salty for fish, but is ideal for floating. Salt water is more buoyant because the molecules of salt and water are joined tightly together. You can see how these tightly-knit molecules hold things up better than loosely linked fresh water molecules by trying to float things in both salt and tap water.

FLOATING FISH

1 To make your fish, cut a 1/2-inch thick slice from a washed, medium-sized potato. Cut a triangular tail fin and a semi-circle from colored cellophane.

1

3

2

2 Get an adult to help you make a slit in the potato circle from the center toward the edge. Push the cellophane semicircle through to make balancing fins. Cut another slit along the potato peel for the tail.

3 To make salty water, drop at least 8 large spoonsful of salt in a plastic bottle three-quarters full of cold water. (Note if there is a change in the water level.) Stir the solution with a straw until no more salt will dissolve.

4 Fill a second plastic bottle with the same amount of water as the salt solution. Pour in a few drops of food coloring. Shake it gently to mix the color well.

4

5 Pour the salt solution into a clear bottle from which the top has been cut. Slowly add the colored water by pouring it over the back of a spoon. Place your fish on the water's surface. It will sink no deeper than the surface of salt water.

WHY IT WORKS

Your fish floats in salt water yet sinks in fresh water. This is because the density of the fish is less than the density of the salt water, but more than the fresh water. When you poured salt crystals into the water, the water level did not go up. Instead the salt dissolved and the mixture filled the same space. Therefore, the density of the liquid increased.

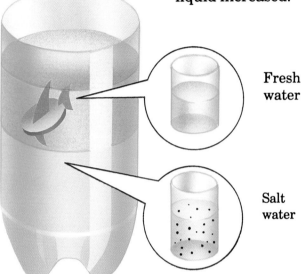

Fresh water

Salt water

BRIGHT IDEAS

You can get the salt back out of the water. Try boiling your solution dry in a saucepan. Be very careful! The salt remains behind. Carefully trap some of the vapor from the boiling solution with the back of a spoon. Watch it condense. The drops of water will be salt-free. Pour all the salt from a salt shaker into a full glass of water. The glass of water will not overflow.

FLOATING LIQUIDS

On a rainy day you will often see oil shimmering on a puddle of water. Like certain objects, liquids, too, can float on other liquids, forming layers as in a salad dressing bottle. Light liquids will float on heavier liquids. Salad oil floats on vinegar because the salad oil is less dense.

Mustard is often added to mix the two solutions as it acts as an emulsifier. Most oils float on water, too. Oil spills can blacken the surface of thousands of miles of water, devastating entire ocean regions and coastlines. One way to disperse a slick and make it mix with water, is to spray it with detergent. You can capture the effect of an oil spill with oil-based paints, water, and paper.

SLICK PICTURES

3 Using a clean stick, swirl the colors around. Do this gently on the water's surface. You can make lots of different patterns. When you have made a pattern that you really like, you are ready to capture it as a picture on white paper.

1

1 To make your oil slick pictures you will need some oil-based paints, thinned with turpentine. Choose bright colors to make exciting prints.

2

3

4

4 Lower one sheet of clean, strong paper on top of the paint. Make sure there are no air bubbles. Allow the paint to soak in for a few minutes. Carefully lift the paper off again. Place it on some newspaper to dry.

2 Fill a deep plastic bowl with cold water. Make sure the bowl is bigger than the sheets of paper you are using for your pictures. (You can add a few drops of vinegar to the water.) Drop small amounts of paint onto the surface of the water.

WHY IT WORKS

Your paints float on the surface because they are less dense than the water below. Liquids of different densities will form into layers in a container, the least dense sitting at the top. To mix the liquids, an emulsifier splits the top layer into tiny droplets that cascade into the layer below. Detergent is an emulsifier that allows oil and water to mix.

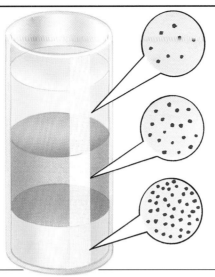

BRIGHT IDEAS

☀ Try pulling the blank paper through the surface paint and wiggling it as you do so. You will have a pattern on both sides of the paper.

☀ Squeeze a few drops of dishwashing liquid onto the surface of the paints. Notice how this changes your marbling pattern.

☀ Pour some oil gently onto the surface of cold water in a screw-top jar. Add dishwashing liquid and shake vigorously. Notice what has happened to the two layers in the jar.

☀ To measure the density of liquids, make an hydrometer with a plastic straw and some modeling clay. Adjust the ball of clay on the bottom of the straw until it will float upright in water. Make a mark on the straw at the surface of the water. Now float it in other liquids and observe the change in levels.

5

5 You can keep making pictures until all the paint is used up. The more pictures you make, the paler the colors will become. Experiment with new designs and colors by dropping more paint onto the surface.

Hydrometer

Water

Other liquid

FLOAT OR SINK?

Enormous aircraft carriers and luxury cruise ships float, yet a single metal screw will sink! Clearly, when it comes to floating, size is not important. Nor necessarily is weight. Whether an object floats or sinks depends on its density and its shape. The Greek mathematician Archimedes noticed that the water level in the bath rose when he got in. He decided that for something to float, the upward push of the water must by the same as the weight of the water displaced, or pushed aside, by the object. Using different objects you can test the rules of floating and sinking.

CRAFTY VESSELS

1 Mold some modeling clay into a solid shape. Try a solid "boat." Drop it into a dish of cold water. Watch it sink to the bottom of the dish. Try other solid shapes, such as a ball.

2 Now use your hands or a rolling pin to roll the clay flat. Curve the edges up to make a boat. Be sure that there are no holes or it will leak!

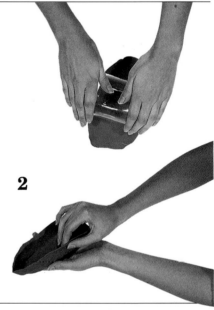

2

1

3 Half fill a shallow dish with cold water. Gently place your boat onto the surface of the water. It will float easily unless there is a leak. Check how low in the water your boat sits. Mark a water level line on the side of the boat. If you want the boat to carry a load safely, it must sit high in the water.

BRIGHT IDEAS

💡 Can you make your boat even more sea-worthy? Mold different shapes. A high-sided shape floats better than a shallow one. Make a long-shaped boat and a round-shaped one. See how many passengers your boat will carry. Try different loads. Mark a safe water level on your craft. This is called a plimsoll line after Samuel Plimsoll.

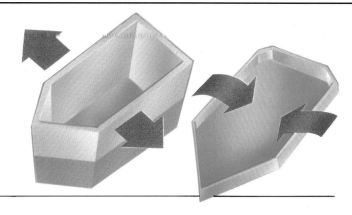

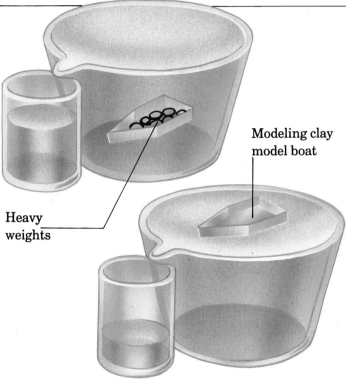

Heavy weights

Modeling clay model boat

WHY IT WORKS

When you dropped a solid piece of clay into the water, it sank. But when you hollowed out the same piece of clay, it floated. This is because by making a boat shape, you changed the density of the solid blob. Solid clay is more dense than water and therefore sinks. But the boat shape holds air which is less dense than water, causing the overall density of the boat to be less dense than the water, thus allowing it to float. An object's shape controls the amount of water it pushes out of the way. If the amount of water pushed aside, or displaced, weighs the same or more than the object, then the object will float. If the amount of water weighs less than the object, it will sink. You can test this by comparing the weights of floating and overloaded boats to the weights of the water they displace.

4

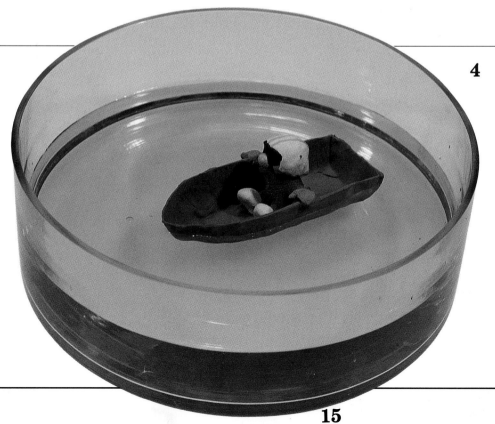

4 Now make a modeling clay passenger. Sit your passenger in the middle of the boat so that it doesn't tip over. (The one shown here is gripping the sides to stay balanced.) Put the boat back in the water and watch it float with the new load. The water level will change. See if it sits lower in the water than the empty boat.

CURVING WATER

A glass of water can be more than full without overflowing. The water seems to puff above the rim of the glass as if held by an invisible skin. Dew drops on a leaf appear to have this skin and so does water at the surface of a still pond. The water strider can glide at great speed over this taut film on the top of water. If you dip the bristles of a paintbrush in water they will spread out. When you lift it out again, they pull together. Each of these effects arise from surface tension, the force between molecules at the surface of all water. You can test its strength yourself.

WATER WALKERS

1 To make your water insects you will need some light-weight aluminum foil and some paper clips. Use sharp scissors to cut the foil into small pieces, one for each paper clip. Make a number of insects so that you can experiment. You can vary the size of your insects.

2 Place a paper clip in the middle of one half of each piece of foil. Fold over the other half of the foil so that the paper clip is enclosed. With your fingers, shape six legs on each insect. Look at the insects in the picture opposite.

3 Half fill a shallow dish with cold water. Very gently lower each insect onto the water's surface.

4. You can position all of your insects on the water at once. To do this you need a paper tissue. Place your insects on the tissue. Holding it firmly at each end, lower the tissue until it rests on the surface of the water.

WHY IT WORKS

Water molecules attract each other. Surface molecules have no water molecules attracting them from above so they pull together extra hard at the sides. The result is a force called surface tension - strong enough to support certain insects. Dishwashing liquid reduces this surface tension by breaking down the forces of attraction between the water molecules.

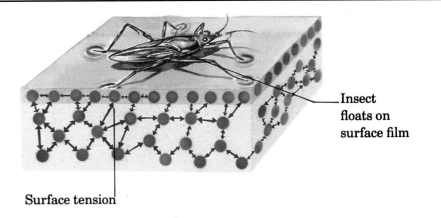

Insect floats on surface film

Surface tension

6 When the water is still, carefully drop some dishwashing liquid onto the surface, just behind each insect. Watch them dart about! To repeat, you need fresh water.

5 The tissue will soak up water and gradually sink to the bottom. But the insects will rest on the surface. Before making your insects dart over the water make sure the liquid is absolutely still.

6

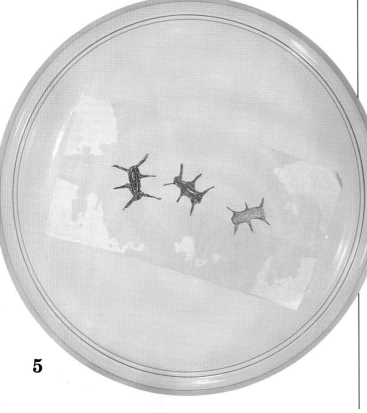

5

BRIGHT IDEAS

Float your insects together in the center of the bowl and carefully drop some dishwashing liquid on the water between them. Watch the skaters dart away.

Sprinkle talcum powder onto a shallow dish full of water. Touch the water in one spot with dishwashing liquid and see what happens.

Dishwashing liquid

RISING ACTION

An invisible force called gravity pulls everything toward the earth. However, there are times when water can flow against this force. Plants and trees contain tubes through which water is drawn upward, carried from the roots to the leaves and flowers. In the same way, flowers in a vase take up water through their stems. This process is called capillary action. You can make a closed paper flower unfurl its petals by using the force of capillary action.

PAPER PETALS

1 Take a square piece of smooth writing paper or thin cardboard and fold it in half lengthwise to make a shape twice as long as it is wide. Do not use shiny paper.

2, 3 Fold your rectangular shape in half so that it forms a square. Now fold your square diagonally to make a triangle.

4 Draw a petal shape on your triangle as shown in the picture. The straight edge is the thickest fold in the paper. Cut out your shape carefully with a pair of sharp scissors. Open it up and you will have a flower.

5 Roll up each petal with a pencil to make each curl tightly. Your flower is now closed up. Make two or three flowers. Experiment with different shapes and sizes.

6 Brighten up your flower by decorating it. This one has a red circle glued in the center.

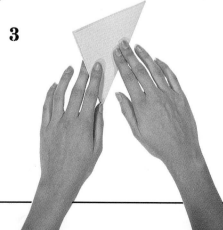

1

2

3

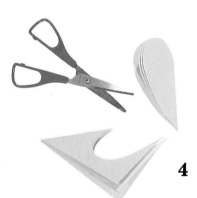

4

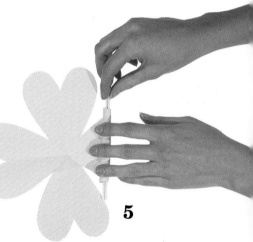

5

6

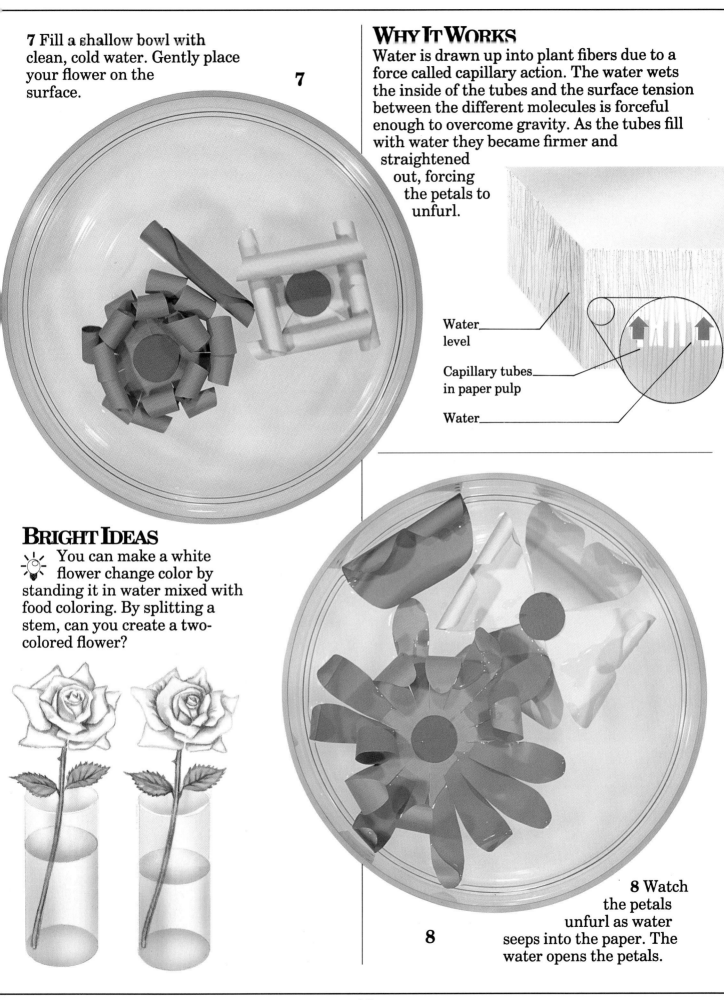

7 Fill a shallow bowl with clean, cold water. Gently place your flower on the surface.

7

WHY IT WORKS

Water is drawn up into plant fibers due to a force called capillary action. The water wets the inside of the tubes and the surface tension between the different molecules is forceful enough to overcome gravity. As the tubes fill with water they became firmer and straightened out, forcing the petals to unfurl.

Water level

Capillary tubes in paper pulp

Water

BRIGHT IDEAS

You can make a white flower change color by standing it in water mixed with food coloring. By splitting a stem, can you create a two-colored flower?

8 Watch the petals unfurl as water seeps into the paper. The water opens the petals.

8

DIVING DEEP

Submarines were once the creation of science fiction. Today, underwater vessels map the ocean floor, repair oil rigs, and fire torpedoes. There is even a home for aquanauts beneath the sea! To dive and resurface, submarines have borrowed their design from nature. Some jellyfish, usually seen at the surface, can sink into the deep by deflating the air sac that aids their propulsion. In the same way, submarine tanks take in water to go down and replace it with air to rise up again. This kind of diving and resurfacing is possible because water is heavier than air, and water-filled objects will always sink. Try it yourself with a jellyfish that takes in water to dive and expels it to resurface.

PLUNGING JELLYFISH

1 To make the jellyfish, you will need a bendable plastic straw, a paper clip and some modeling clay. Bend the ribbed part of the straw and cut the long side to the same length as the short side.

1

2 Bend a paper clip as shown here. Insert the bent paper clip into each end of the straw. Push the paper clip firmly inside, making sure that it will not slide out.

2

3 Roll out three thin strips of clay. Loop and pinch each one around the paper clip.

3

4

4 Test your jellyfish in a clear cup of water to make sure that it will float the right side up. If it doesn't, try adding more clay. This will give it weight and balance. Place it to sit as shown here.

5 Float your jellyfish in a large bottle full of water. Screw on the top.

5

20

WHY IT WORKS

When you squeeze the bottle, water is pushed into the plastic straw, compressing the air. Because water weighs more than air, the jellyfish gets heavier, causing it to sink.

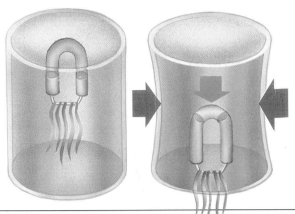

BRIGHT IDEAS

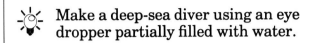

Instead of using a screw-top bottle, try using a deep plastic container to house your jellyfish. Stretch plastic wrap over the top and secure with a rubber band. Apply some pressure to the cling film. Which works best?

Make a deep-sea diver using an eye dropper partially filled with water.

Try floating a plastic bottle filled with varying amounts of water. Try filling it half full or three-quarters full. See how easy it is to submerge with these different amounts of water.

6 Squeeze the sides of the plastic bottle hard. The jellyfish will sink to the bottom as water enters the straw, compressing the air inside it. This makes the jellyfish heavier.

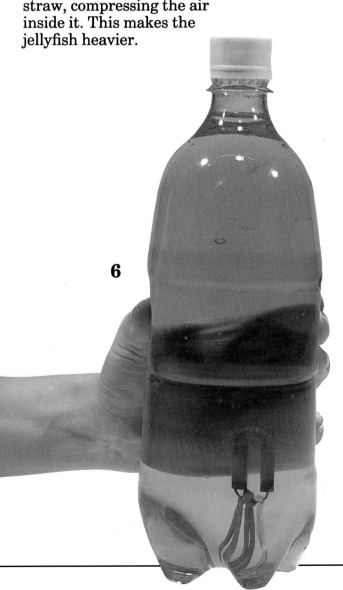

6

7 Releasing the pressure on the sides of the bottle allows the jellyfish to rise to the surface again. The compressed air inside the straw expands again, forcing the water back out. The jellyfish becomes lighter and therefore more buoyant.

7

HYDRAULIC MUSCLE

Water can be made to lift heavy things. Because water and other liquids cannot be squeezed, if they are thrust through pipes, they will carry a powerful force. In the 17th century, Blaise Pascal was the first person to discover the principles of hydraulics. Hydraulic lifts are machines that use the natural pushing power of liquids to raise loads. Most modern hydraulic lifts use oil instead of water. Excavating machines operate hydraulic rams. Cars have hydraulic brakes. In the 1930's, the fire services reached greater heights by introducing hydraulically operated turntable ladders. Today, disabled skiers make use of a hydraulic skibob with hydraulic suspension. You can make your own hydraulic lift simply by linking two water-filled containers.

LIQUID LIFT

1 Using sharp scissors, carefully cut the tops off two bottles. Make them the same height.

2 Pierce a hole in the side of each bottle about 2 inches from the bottom. Link the two bottles by inserting the plastic straw into the holes. Use the clay as a seal; there should be no leaks when the bottles are filled with water.

3 You need a balloon, a plastic cup, and some clay. Place the clay inside the cup.

4 Fill the bottles with cold water to the level shown in the picture, about three-quarters full. You can add food coloring to see the water levels more clearly. Place the weighted cup on the surface of the water in one of the containers. Experiment with different weights of clay. It must float. This will be your load.

22

WHY IT WORKS

Unlike air, liquids cannot be compressed, or squeezed; any pressure that is applied to them passes through the liquid in every direction without loss of strength. When you push down on one side of your water lift, the water has no place to go but up the other side. Pressure from the rising water raises the load.

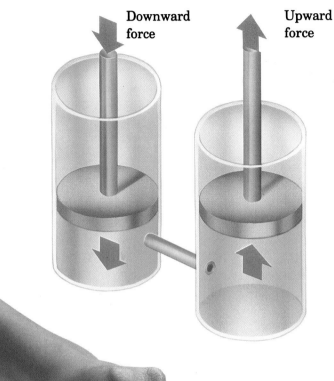

Downward force

Upward force

BRIGHT IDEAS

💡 Increase the load to be lifted. Try several different weights. Test to see if they can be raised as high as each other. Push the balloon down to the same level every time!

💡 Now make a different type of water lift. Replace one bottle with a taller, narrower bottle. See if a load in this new bottle can be raised higher. Notice what happens if you put the load in the other side.

💡 Try making an oil lift. Pour the water out of both containers and replace it with cooking oil. Does this lift work as well or better than the water lift? Oil is messy stuff, so be sure to clean up thoroughly!

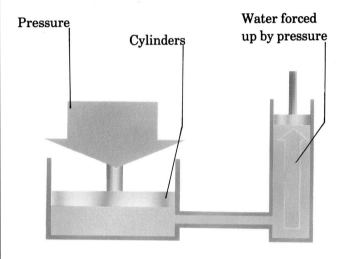

Pressure

Cylinders

Water forced up by pressure

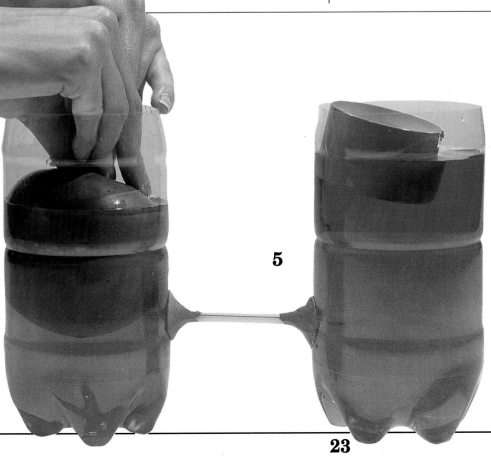

5

5 Position the inflated balloon on the surface of the water and gently push it down. As you push the water down on one side it rises up the other side, lifting the load. The balloon acts as a piston. To raise the load even higher, you need to put more pressure on the balloon. Note the water levels in both bottles. If the water under the balloon goes down by a certain amount, observe how far it goes up on the other side.

SOARING FOUNTAINS

Water naturally flows downhill. The pull of gravity draws it down as low as possible. To spurt upward, like the fountain pictured here, water must be put under pressure. When hot rock from the earth's core superheats underground water, a hot, steamy fountain called a geyser bursts skyward. Old Faithful in Yellowstone National Park, rises 150 feet into the air every 70 minutes because of this pressure. A natural fountain will only rise as high as the water table that it feeds. Some natural fountains are fed by water from high lakes. You can make a fountain and also prove that water pressure increases with depth by building the two projects shown here.

LIQUID JETS

1 You need a plastic soda bottle, two plastic straws, a plastic tray, and some modeling clay. Cut off the bottom of the bottle.

2 Seal the mouth closed with modeling clay. Poke a straw through it as shown. Fit another straw to the end of the first one.

3 Pierce two holes in the plastic tray, one at each end of the base. Turn the bottle upside down and feed straws through the holes. Seal the bottle in position with clay. Also secure the free end of the straw to the tray in the same way.

4 Place the tray and bottle inside a shallow container. Half fill the bottle with water. The pressure of this reservoir will cause a fountain to spurt through the straw if there are no airlocks in the straw.

1

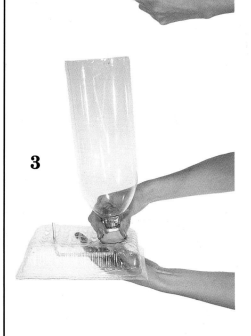

2

3

4

BRIGHT IDEAS

Add more water to the reservoir. What do you notice about the height of the jet from your fountain?

You can prove that the pressure of water increases with depth. Cut the top off a plastic bottle and make holes at different levels along one side. Put the bottle in a deep-sided dish. With your fingers, cover the holes and have a friend pour water in the bottle. When the bottle is full release your fingers. See how water pressure from above forces longer jets of water through the lower holes.

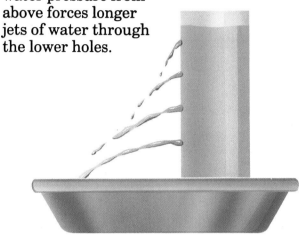

WHY IT WORKS

Pressure from the water in your fountain reservoir pushes the water through the straw, causing it to leap into the air. The deeper you fill the reservoir, the greater the water pressure becomes and the higher the water will shoot up, striving to get as high as the water source.

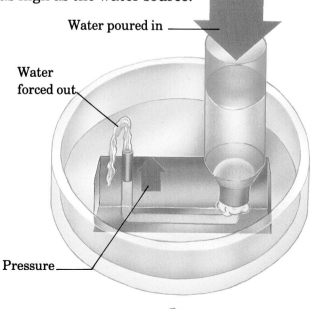

Water poured in

Water forced out

Pressure

WATER ENGINEERING

For thousands of years people have used water's pushing power to drive machines. Since Roman times wooden waterwheels have powered millstones to grind corn. Later, waterwheels became the main power source for industry. One of the largest machines in the world, the modern water turbine, was developed from the waterwheel. Water turbines are harnessed to generators to produce hydroelectric power. With all waterwheels, the flow of water is directed around wheel blades to start the wheel spinning. The constant movement from the revolving wheel can then be put to work. You can make a waterwheel go to work for you. This one raises a bucketful of water.

WATER ENGINEERING

2

1 Cut the bottom from a dishwashing liquid bottle to make a waterwheel. Cut out 4 evenly-spaced flaps around the sides of the bottle and fold them out as shown.

1

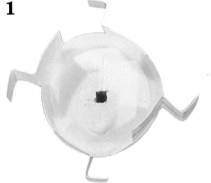

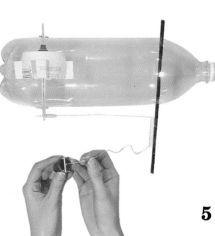

4

2 Make a hole in the base of the waterwheel and insert a straw. Secure it in place with clay. Cut a section from a soda bottle large enough for the waterwheel to sit inside. Pierce two holes on either side of the bottle for the straw to pass through.

5 Make a bucket from a bottle cap. Glue a matchstick across the top. Tie it to thread.

3

3 Fit the waterwheel into the cutout section of the bottle, easing the straw through the holes. Poke toothpicks through the straw to secure it in place.

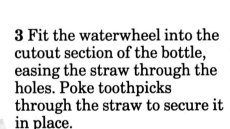

4 Make two holes through the top of the bottle and insert a pencil or chopstick. Tape a short piece of straw to the end of the pencil.

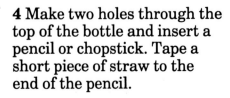

5

6 Feed the thread through the short straw on the pencil and tie it to the waterwheel straw. Cut the base off a dishwashing liquid container. Join it upside down to the soda bottle with clay, making sure the top is off. Stand the whole thing inside a large bowl. Now fill the detergent bottle with water. Watch the waterwheel work as the falling water hits the blades. It will raise the "bucket" for you.

6

BRIGHT IDEAS

Test the power of your waterwheel with a heavier load. Try putting a small weight in the bucket. See what happens when you increase the force of the water falling onto the wheel. Suspend the wheel beneath the water flow from a sink. Find the spot where you must hold it to make it turn faster.

Water

Wheel

WHY IT WORKS

The water creates its own pressure due to its weight. Energy from the fast-flowing water turns your waterwheel, in turn raising the bucket. If you pour water onto the wheel from a great height, the wheel spins faster than if the water falls from just above the blades. This is because water releases more stored energy as it falls.

Water

Blades

PADDLE POWER

The first paddles used for moving vessels in water were probably simple oars. By the early nineteenth century the first steam-powered ships were fitted with paddles. As the paddle circled around and around, it pushed back the water with its blades. This action propelled the vessel forward. It was Isaac Newton who first stated that for every action, such as the paddle pushing against the water, there is an equal and opposite reaction – the vessel being propelled forward. The British engineer Isambard Kingdom Brunel built the first iron ship to be driven by a screw propeller which, like the paddle, pushes the water backward and the ship forward. Today, paddle steamers, like the one pictured here, still carry tourists on the Mississippi River. You can make a model boat that is powered the same way.

SPEEDY BOATS

1 Take a small plastic bottle with a top and cut a hole in one side large enough for a cardboard tube. This cardboard tube will be the funnel of your paddle steamer.

2 Tape two sticks or pencils on either side of the bottle. They should stick out about 2 inches past the bottom of the bottle.

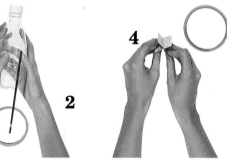

3 Cut two rectangles from a fruit juice carton. Make sure they are smaller than the base of the bottle.

4 Make a slit halfway down the middle of each. Slide them together to form a paddle.

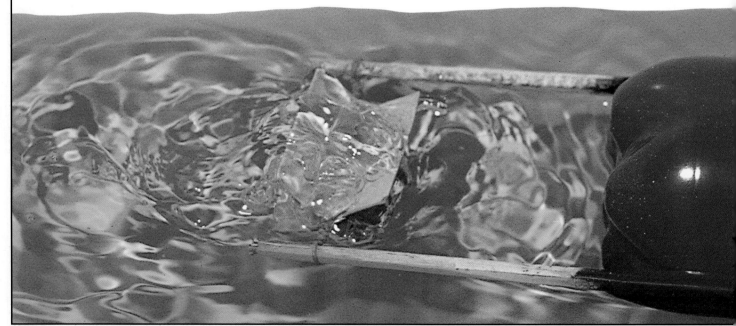

WHY IT WORKS

The paddleboat is driven by the potential, or hidden, energy stored in the rubber band. As the rubber band unwinds, the paddle turns, pushing the water backward and the boat forward. The potential energy has been changed into kinetic, or moving, energy.

BRIGHT IDEAS

Find out how far the boat travels in relation to the number of turns that you give the paddle. You can make a graph to show the results. See if winding up the paddle in or out of the water makes any difference.

Twist the paddle clockwise and note what happens when the boat moves. Now twist it counterclockwise. Attach a different rubber band to your boat. Notice if a tighter rubber band changes the boat's motion.

Make a propeller-driven boat. See if it goes farther or faster than a paddle-driven boat. Race your two different types of boat together in the bathtub.

6 Place the paddle wheel in between the sticks. Loop the ends of the rubber band around each stick. Make sure that the paddle wheel is not touching the bottle.

7

7 Weight the boat down with clay. Fit a cardboard tube in the hole. Wind up the paddle around the rubber band and place the boat in the water. Let go and watch it shoot forward.

6

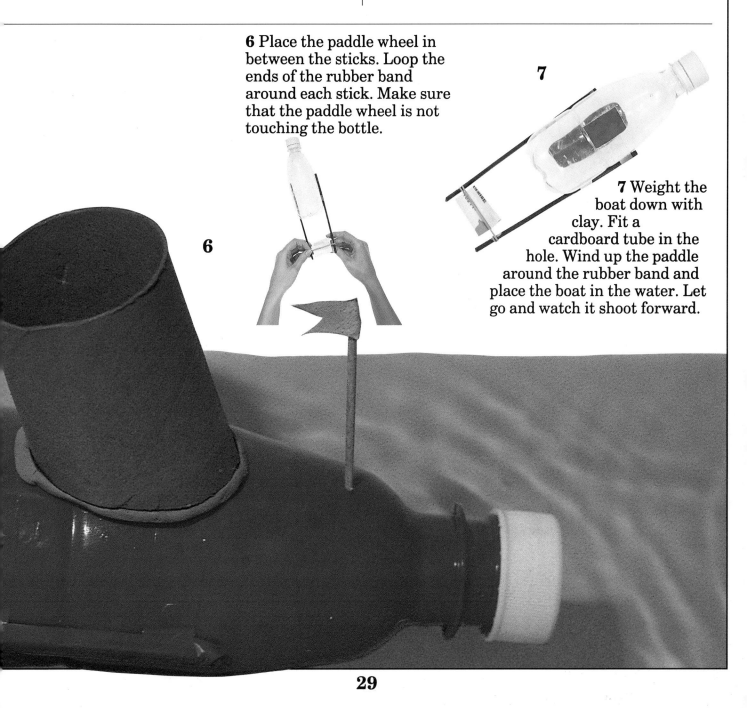

STEERING AND BALANCE

The Vikings used a single, hand-operated steering oar at the stern, or back, of their ships. Always on the right-hand side, it led to the term steerboard, or starboard. Stern rudders were first used over 1,000 years ago on flat-bottomed Chinese junks. Modern propeller-driven submarines are steered by tail rudders. To maneuver up and down, they use hydroplane fins which look like airplane wings. Dolphins are propelled by their tail fins – the other fins are for balance and steering.

RUDDER DESIGN

1 For your rudder, slide a pipe cleaner inside a straw, leaving a piece sticking out at the top for the handle and a piece at the bottom.

2 Cut out the shape for the rudder from a fruit juice container. Attach it to the straight end of the pipe cleaner. Make sure it points in the opposite direction to the handle.

3 Attach the finished rudder to the back of your paddleboat with modeling clay. Wind the paddle counterclockwise to propel the boat through the water. Once it is moving, use the handle of the rudder to change the direction in which it travels. Keep a record of what happens. When you push the handle to the right, observe which way the rudder turns. At the same time, notice which way this makes the boat turn.

3

BRIGHT IDEAS

💡 If you want to turn the boat to starboard, which way must you turn the rudder? See if you can make your boat do a complete turn by operating the rudder.

💡 Make a "submarine" and fit four adjustable curved fins to the sides. To maneuver, or turn, your vessel, experiment with the fins. With the back fins and the front fins curving in the same direction, gently drop the submarine in water. Now test what happens when the fins are fixed in different directions. For example, try the front fins curving up and the back fins curving down.

WHY IT WORKS

If the rudder is pointing in the same direction as the flow of water, the ship moves straight ahead (3). If the flow strikes the rudder at an angle (1,2), the ship turns. As the force of the flow tries to push the angled rudder back to parallel, it is met with resistance - an opposing force that turns the boat.

1

2

3

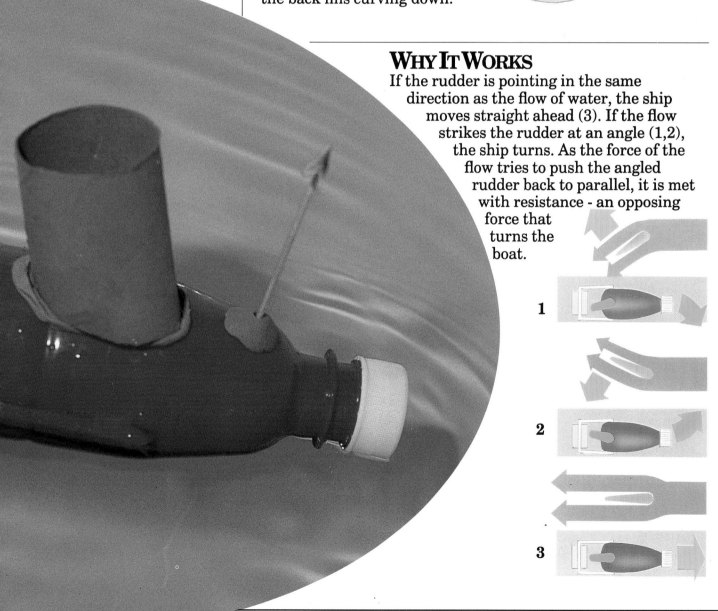

Scientific Terms

AQUANAUT A person who works, swims, or dives underwater

BOILING POINT 212 F – The temperature at which water turns to steam

CAPILLARY ACTION The rising or falling of water in contact with a solid

CONDENSATION The change of a gas, such as water vapor, into liquid drops

DENSITY The heaviness of a substance for a particular volume

EVAPORATION The change of a liquid to a gas by the escape of molecules from its surface

HYDRAULICS The technology of liquids in motion and at rest

HYDROMETER An instrument for measuring the relative density of liquids

MENISCUS The curved surface of water in a tube, produced by surface tension

MOLECULE The smallest naturally occurring particle of

a substance

PLIMSOLL LINE A load line painted on the hull of a ship

SALINITY Saltiness

SURFACE TENSION The molecular force of a liquid that pulls it into the smallest possible area, making water drops round and forming a meniscus in a glass of water

WATER VAPOR The gas evaporated from the surface of liquid water. (Vapor from boiling water is called steam.)

Index

PRINTED IN BELGIUM BY

INTERNATIONAL BOOK PRODUCTION

MA